WHO I AM IN CHRIST

BETTY S DELCAMBRE

Acknowledgments

I would like to give praise and glory to our Lord Jesus Christ for calling upon me to prophesy His word. *But one who prophesies strengthens others, encourages them, and comforts them. 1 Corinthian 14:3.* I pray to have honored Him in my understanding and my explanation of who He says "I am" in my identity. He has been guiding me throughout the progression of this book, giving and taking intel that it became what He had created in His image. He is the true author, I am only His sheep, His instrument. He was very persistent when calling on me to be obedient in this journey. When I finally understood He was calling me for this assignment, I found myself along with one of my sons in a local drive-through sharing His word with a stranger. A true push of encouragement, God knew I needed to fulfill His call. I give all the praise and glory to my Father, for He is the true author; He gets all the credit. *My sheep listen to my voice; I know them, and they follow me. I give them eternal life, they will never perish no one can snatch them away from me. John* 10:27-28

With true love and honor, I dedicate this book to my Husband of twenty-seven years. He has not only supported me along the divine assignment that God has given me to conduct in a manner He has instructed. Fulfilling this assignment took considerable amounts of reassurance of my confidence by my husband. When I did not believe in myself, He encouraged me to believe what God says about me is true. When I doubted myself in my faith and ability to prophesy God's word, He was by my side to discuss the challenges I was facing. He would remind me that God called me on this journey, and He will lead me if I ask him. With encouraging words, He would remind me to make quiet time for the Lord so that I could hear Him and be able to receive His words. I thank you for believing in me through my journey from the beginning when receiving the gifts of prophecy, wisdom, and understanding from the Holy Spirit. For your encouragement to grow in each gift I received, I will forever be grateful. You have been a great spiritual companion in the renewal of my faith and in our newfound friendship and marriage in Christ.

Dedications

To my sons for always believing in me as a daughter of God. For always loving and supporting me in all my obstacles through your lives. For being proud to call me your mom. You all truly motivate and inspire me to be the best form of myself. Each one of you are true blessings in my life. Not only because you make me smile, you each have filled my heart with happiness. *Children are a gift from the Lord they are a reward from Him Romans 126:3*

To my daughters-in-law-to-be, I am honored that God chose you both to join our family. I love you both for the faith, love, and desire in your hearts. For the support you have given me, and of course, the granddaughters you both allow me to love unconditionally.

To my parents, I thank you both for guiding me from birth along my journey in choosing God as my savior. To love my faith and to believe what God says about me is true. *Honor your father and mother that the days may be long in the land that the Lord your God is giving you. Exodus 20:12*

To my siblings, in-laws, nieces, nephews, godchildren, sisters, and brothers in Christ, thank you all for praying, loving, supporting, and believing in me as a child of God.

To my Bestie and niece for listening to me daily on my journey. For sharing words of confidence when I was at my lowest and tough love when I wanted to give up. Thank you for accepting my long-winded talks when I was on a high of the Holy Spirit. Praying for me without me asking. You are both my rock of confidence, love, and true support that any girl would love to endure. Thank you for loving me and for my dedication to God Our Father. You both have always supported me in life, and I will forever be in debt to you.

The Lord has done it this very day let us rejoice today and be glad. Psalm 118:24

The Author/God's Instrument

Writing my introduction would have looked so different just months ago. I would have gone on about my husband, mama boys, daughter-inlaws-to-be, and my adorable granddaughters. The signs we receive from our baby girl in Heaven. Even though I am still enormously proud to carry all these titles and wear them proudly, my Identity has changed from being a wife, mother, Nana, and mother-in-law, to the greatest identity of all, a Child of God.

I am a daughter of Our Almighty Father, the highest King of Kings and Lord of Lords. I am a believer, I am born again, I am on fire for our savior, I am courageous, accepted, rescued, valuable, a work in progress, I am a sinner, I am wonderfully made. I am a born and raised catholic.

I have attended the same church in my hometown for the majority of my life. I have always strived to show the ways of the catholic faith to my husband and boys and now my granddaughters and daughters-in-law-to-be. Rebuilding my faith in the Lord, and building my relationship with my best friend, my savior, as it slowly slipped away over the years. I let life take over and lost my identity in my faith.

Attending my first catholic retreat as an adult would leave me wanting to become who God calls me to be. When I was prayed over, at which time I received the gifts of prophecy, wisdom, and understanding from the Holy Spirit and received blessings of freedom, love, and encouragement. I started a bible study monthly in my home. I attended an Encounter School of Ministry Conference with two extraordinarily strong, faithful ladies. The conference was an indescribable, true, breath-taking life experience. I have not at all missed my earlier life before becoming a true Child of God. I took a summer catholic ministry class, which left me seeking more of His wisdom.

Now, I am attending a two-year ministry class. The more I receive the word of God, the more I want to live more like Him and less like who I see myself as. *He must become greater and greater, and I must become less and less. John 3:30*

I give Him glory for never leaving my side, even when I would get off the path He cleared for me. For never giving up on me, for always walking alongside me. He gave me free will to choose to get back on the path He created for me to travel. I am a small-town catholic daughter of Christ. I strive to give Him praise and glory in all that I am and all that I do.

As a daughter of God, He fully and completely accepts me. Knowing this does not mean I am perfect and that I never seek acceptance from others. Knowing who I am in Christ keeps me humbled. I am reminded that my identity is rooted in Him alone and not through the eyes of others.

Today, I challenge you to commit to seeking your identity in Jesus Christ, Our Lord and Savior.

INTRODUCTION

Threw-out this book, bible verses will be inserted to support His words. He calls for us to study verses and to journal our thoughts, growing our faith. Personal stories from my journey in hopes of encouraging others along theirs. Sharing testimonies may be encouraging for others, they may receive peace, comfort, and assurance when needing them most. Activities to help you reflect in prayer, asking God what it is He wants you to take from the contents provided. A Helpful list to guide you in growing your knowledge in your faith. Prayers and different ideas on how to pray to receive Our Lord's message. Created in His image, we are all God's Children. Pray to be totally accepted in becoming more like Him and less like who you and others say you are. Not every activity, bible verse, or my personal stories will inspire everyone. But through you, they may mean something to someone else. I have prayed for understanding and guidance to be shared from my deliverance of His word. I have prayed for the truth of who God says we are to be completely present in our hearts, minds, and souls.

Reflective Prayer Exercise

I want to share the ways through which I grew in my prayer life throughout my journey. Prehab's ways you will adopt in your own prayer life. The crucial point is to find your own prayer posture.

Choose a nice, comfortable, quiet place within your home or even outdoors. Make this space all your own for your time with Jesus. Turn off all distractions and invite Jesus in. Be available for Holy Silence so God can sit with you and talk with you.

Ask Him to quiet your mind, thoughts, and steal your heart; be completely present in this time with him. *In returning and rest you shall be saved: in quietness and in trust shall be your strength Isaiah 30:15*

Sit quietly, take slow, deep breaths, ask God to forgive you for your sins and that you can forgive those who have trespassed against you. Give Him thanks for all the answered and unanswered prayers. Always give Him praise and glory.

Give thanks to the Lord for He is good His mercy endures forever. Psalm 118:1

Committing to this time shows Him that you are obedient in your relationship with Him. You will learn to hear His voice. You will have to persevere and not give up on Him or yourself. Keep pressing; He wants this relationship more than you do. He just wants to be shown our commitment to Him is true. He waited patiently my whole life through all my pain and sorrows for me to be obedient to him, for me to hear His voice. Looking back now, if only I had trusted completely in Him when we lost our baby girl or when my identity in the eyes of others was destroyed by one person. The more I sit and talk with Him, the more I hear His voice and the stronger the presents of The Holy Spirit I encounter.

Once you have invited Him in, give Him praise and glory, repent your sins and sit still, know He is with you. Talk to him, share with Him everything that is heavy on your heart, sit quietly, and listen. He will answer. Be Still,

Be Quiet, and Be Alone with your best friend. Do not check out! A soul that has lost the desire for silence has lost its desire to hear Jesus's voice. *I will give thanks to the Lord with my whole heart: I will tell of all your wonderful deeds.* Psalm 9:1

From the Beginning

Before we get started on your journey of finding your identity in Christ, take time to reflect on yourself.

For the first exercise, recall all things from your life that you believe define who you are. Have an open mind when completing this exercise. Do this activity from your current mind set. How do you see yourself at this moment. Date it so that you reflect on how far you have grown in your journey with Christ.

Use my trunk to list the ways in which you define yourself.

Use my water to describe the things you do throughout your daily life that define you.

Use my branches to describe all your possessions that form your identity.

Helpful Tips

Seek the kingdom of God and His
righteousness. and all those things shall be added to you.
Matthew 6:38

Four types of prayers that could help strengthen your prayer time.

1. Ignatian Prayer- imaginative, reflective, and personal imagination to bring scripture to life.

2. Augustinian prayer- practical application of the scripture, reading and pulling out of it, whatever you find that applies to your present circumstances.

3. Franciscan prayer- carefree, moving impulsively to what the Spirit is calling you to receive.

4. Thomistic prayer- neat and orderly intellectual prayer life, study the word from every angle: who, what, when, why, and how.

Ways to grow in finding your Identity in Christ

- Repent your sins, forgive others, Ask for forgiveness.

- Rejoice, give God all the praise and glory for answered prayers and unanswered prayers. The no's make room for an improved Yes.

- Receive the gifts of our Lord Jesus Christ, The Body and Blood of Jesus.

- Embrace The "Bride" of Christ, The Holy Catholic Church.

- Pray in His holy name, for what we ask in His holy name, we are granted.

- Believe in what you pray for. We cannot receive in what we do not believe.

- To be more like Him and less like who you and others say you are.

- Pray for others. Pray with others.

- Pray for boldness and confidence in spreading His word.

- Educate your heart, mind, and soul.

- Read the Holy Bible, break it down, and study the verses.

- Hearing and seeing His word strengthens our faith.

- Memorizing scripture encourages and strengthens our foundation.

- A solid foundation to stand firm on encourages us to share His word.

- Faith-Based Books give understanding from the knowledge, wisdom, and testimonies of others. Helping us grow stronger and more submersed in our faith.

- Hear His word in worship music, daily mass, podcasts, and daily devotions.

- Share the word of the Lord, share kind words, share a smile, share a helping hand.

- Through learning more of His word, by seeing, hearing, and sharing, we grow deeper in our Faith. We start to look more like Jesus and less like our appearance.

- Trust fully in your Lord Jesus Christ.

- Talk with him, He is your best friend.

- Trust in His word, His promises.

- Give Him all your worries, miss beliefs, pains, and sorrows.

- Keep a prayer journal, making sure to date it. Reflect on how God has worked in your life.

- Make a list of promises to yourself and God, things to change, and things to grow stronger in Him. Free up room to have time and do Godly things for others.

- Keep a journal of the signs and words you receive from God.

- Write testimonies for events that help form you as a Child of God.

- God says, our tears heal, so do not hold them back. He is in control, He turns them on and off as He sees fit.

- Do not text more than you pray. Have no other God.

- We do not always receive for which we pray. We receive what aligns with His Master Plan for our lives. He gives us everything we need to live out His plan. Trust that God knows the best timing for your prayers to be answered.

His faithfulness and promises knowing He is working all
things together for your good.

Romans 8:28

Reflection for busy days.

Seek Him first, Choose Him first, Love Him first,
Obey Him first, Follow Him first, Worship Him first.

Personal prayers I have written to grow in my prayer journey.

Here I am Lord

I come to you and give you complete access. To transform me and be the person you created me to be.

I come willing to accept, all challenges, and obstacles that will come my way. I come laying all my sins, at the foot of the cross, in prayer for forgiveness.

I come and make myself all yours. Available only for you.

I come to you Lord.

Virgin Mother Mary

I come to you for your protection.

I come to you to be my intercessor.

I come to you for your patience.

I come to you for your quietness.

I come to you for your motherly guidance.

I come to you for your warm touch.

I come to you for your Motherly Love.

Our Heavenly Mother is our personal intercessor and takes our prayers straight to the foot of her Almighty Son.

Personal Prayer Activity

On the following page, write a prayer, poem, or reflection of your own. Just short lines or a page long. Reflect on it as you take your journey in the renewal of your faith with Our Lord Jesus Christ. This is your personal prayer. Cherish it, pray it, memorize it. **Date**. Remember, we always invite Him into prayer with us and praise Him. We ask Him for forgiveness and thank Him for the big and small blessings. Ask Him for special intentions in His Holy name, and pray with Him for others.

I will give thanks to the Lord because of His righteousness I will sing the praises of the name of the Lord Most High. Psalm 7:17

Use the following list to help you find and understand your identity.

Ask yourself these questions as you read along.

Who am I? What do I have? What do I do?

The Proper Alignment of Our Identity is I am, I have, I do.

I am a temple	Corinthian 3:16
I am a vessel	2 Timothy 2:2
I am chosen	Ephesians 1:4
I am beloved	Romans 1:7
I am complete in Him	Colossians 2:10
I am free from sins power	Romans 6:14
I am loved eternally	1 Peter 1:5
I am one with the Lord	1 Corinthihians 6:17
I am on my way to Heaven	John 14:6
I am Forgiven	Colossian 1:13-14
I am Jesus Friend	John 15:15
I am a new person	2 Corinthians 5:16-17
I am Fruitful	John 15:5
I am Priceless	Luke 12:6-7
I am child of God	Galatians 3:26

I have enough	2 Corinthians 12:9-10
I have Access	Roman 5:2
I have a heavenly home	John 14:1-2
I have peace	Romans 5:1
I have a soul anchored in the Lord	Hebrew 6:19
I have boldness	Hebrews 10:19
I have all things in Christ	2 Corinthians 5:17
I have wisdom	Ephesians 1:8
I have been redeemed	Revelation 5:9
I have citizenship to Heaven	Philippians 2:25
I have Courage	Deuteronomy 31:6
I have peace	Romans 5:1
I have access to God	James 1:5
I have been Adopted	Ephesians 1:5
I have Righteousness	Roman 5:19
I have purpose	Jeremiah 29.11

I do rein in life	Romas 5:17
I do forgive others	Ephesians 1:17
I do delight in the Lord	Zephaniah 3:17
I do co-labor	1 Corinthians 3:9
I do hold secured in my faith	Jeremiah 29:11
I do Love	Romans 8:39
I do rest in the Lord	Philippians 1:6
I do light the world	John 6:12
I do live in freedom	Roman 8:2
I do have a purpose	Ephesians 2:10
I do sit with Christ.	Ephesians 2:6
I do partake in divine nature	2 Peter 1:4
I do lead by spirit	Romans 8:14
I do cast all my cares on the Lord	1 Peter 5:7
I do exercise authority	Luke 10:19
I do show Gods word	Matthew 16:19

The Beginning

Do you believe that a human being created Heaven and Earth? What about all the living creatures? The mountain tops, rivers, lakes, trees, and flowers? Who do you say the creator of all living things is to you? To me, He is our one and only creator, God The Father Almighty.

In the beginning God created the Heavens and Earth. Genesis 1:1 Then God said 'Let there be light. Genesis 1:3 Let the waters beneath the sky flow together into one place so dry ground may appear. Genesis 1:9 Let lights appear in the sky to separate the day from night. Genesis 1:14 Let the waters swarm with fish and other life. Let the skies be filled with birds of every kind. Genesis 20 Let the earth produce each offspring of the same kind of livestock, small animal that scurry along ground and wild animals. Genesis 24 Let us make human beings in our image to like us. Genesis 26 So God created human beings in His own image in the image of God He created them male and female. Genesis 27 God blessed them and said Be fruitful and multiply fill the earth and govern it. Reign over the fish in the sea, the birds in the sky and all the animals that scurry along the grounds. Genesis 28 Then God looked over all He had made, and He saw that it was exceptionally good. Genesis 31

Create a Masterpiece

God has created all things for us, and He created them exceptionally. Fill in the picture to summarize how you see God's creations. Show the love you receive from becoming a Child of God. Express gratitude through your creation, for He is your Father. He not only created Heaven and Earth, but He also created all things, and He created them exceptionally good.

Salvation is not a reward for the good things we have done, so none of us can boast about it. For we are God's masterpiece. He has created us anew in Christ Jesus, so we can do the good things He planned for us long ago. Ephesians 2:9-10

Gods Creation

God Our Father, the Creator of Heaven and Earth, is the King of the universe. He is our Father. He adopted us as His sons and daughters.

So, you have not received a spirit that makes you fearful slaves. Instead, you received God's Spirit when He adopted you as His own children. Now we call Him Abba, Father. Romans 8:15. He has chosen each of us and has a special grand plan for our lives. He did not ask us if we wanted to choose Him when He created us.

Ye have not chosen me, but I have chosen you, and ordained you, that ye should go and bring forth fruit, and that your fruit should remain that whatsoever ye shall ask of the Father in my name, He may give it you." John 15:16

Even before He made the world God loved us and chose us in Christ to be holy and without fault in His eyes. Ephesian 1:4.

When God created us, choosing us, He made a promise to never leave us alone. He will never leave our sides, no matter the number of times we turn our back on Him. When He adopted us into His Holy Family, as Children of God, we received heritages from Him, the same way we will from our earthly father.

Because of our faith Christ has brought us into this place of underserved privilege where we now stand, and we confidently and joyfully look forward to sharing Gods glory. Romans 5:2. We have been granted access to everything we will ever need to fulfill His calling for us. God has great intentions and big plans for each of us. He has given us free will to make our own decisions, guiding us to choose the righteous path. Even when we stray, He continually shows us the way back to the path He has paved in gold for us. The Father is our protector, and He grants us access to Christ.

That is why I said that people cannot come to me, unless the father gives them to me. John 6:65

The Son gives us eternal life, He is our example of how God calls us to live. *I give them eternal life and they will never perish No one can swatch them away from me.* John *10:28* The Holy Spirit guides us into the truth and names us children of God. *Pilate brought Jesus out to them again, The Pilate sat down on judgment seat, on platform, that is called the stone Pavement. John 19:13*

God gives this and much more through The Father, The Son, and The Holy Spirit. The Trinity.

God the Almighty Father, Son, and Holy Spirit is one in three persons. He oversees and empowers, The Trinity to conduct His will in Heaven and on Earth. Everything that is divine comes through the Trinity and is received by each of His chosen ones.

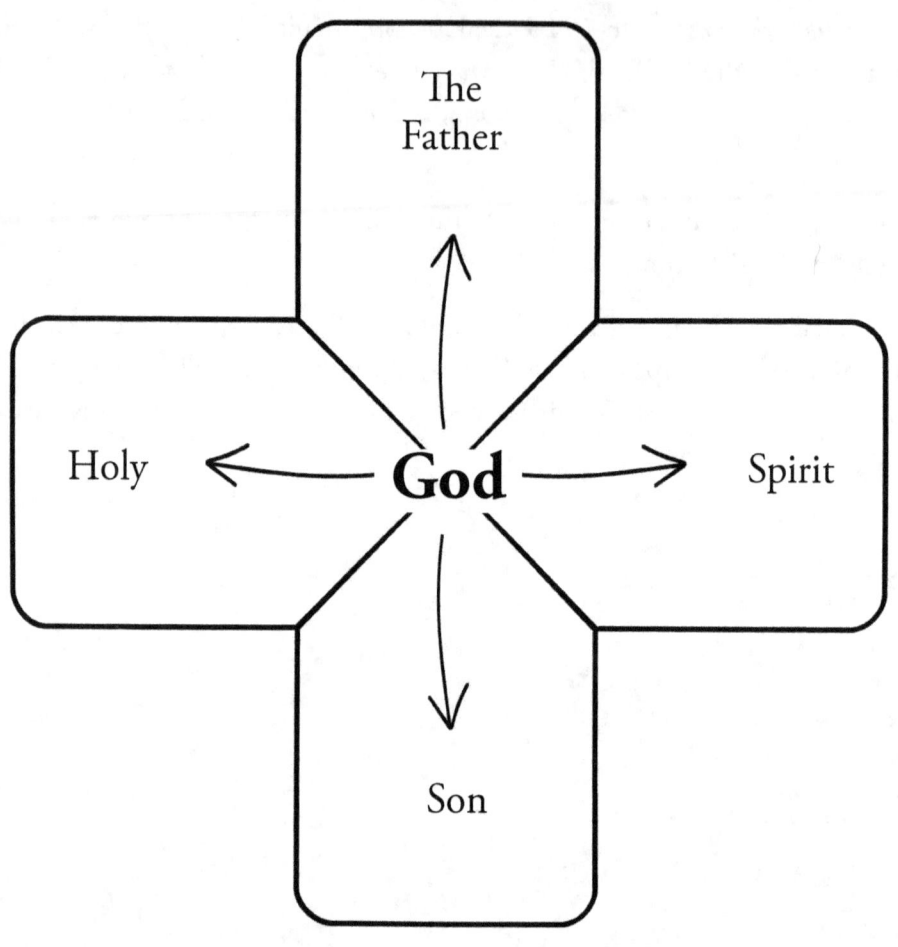

The Father is not, The Son.

The Son is not, The Holy Spirit.

The Holy Spirit is not, The Father.

God is The Father, The Son, The Holy Spirit.

Jesus is the Son of God and the Holy Virgin Mother Mary. Mother Mary is our ultimate example of receiving the word of God. She listened, received, and pondered deeply the words spoken to her. Even though she may not have fully understood, she held these words in her heart, allowing them to grow and take form as our Lord. His flesh has now become our daily bread. He lives as our example. *For God called you to do good even if it means suffering, just as Christ suffered for you. He is your example, and you must follow in His steps, 1 Peter 2:21* He forgives our sins. *Who purchased our freedom and forgave our sins. Colossians 1:14.* Jesus was crucified, He died, a sinner's death, and was buried. He descended into hell for all earthly sins. He rose from the dead and now sits at the right hand of God, our Father Almighty. Jesus lived a human life; He felt pain, He bled, He hungered, He thirsted, and He was faced with temptations of sin. He lived every moment with complete devotion and belief in our God, His Father. Jesus was so obedient to God that He only did what He saw God do and only said what He heard God say. We should strive to live with the same obedience that Jesus had for His Father. We are called to obey Jesus, God, the Holy Spirit, and Mother Mary, just as Jesus obeyed. Try living as Jesus did for a week—do for others as He would, and treat others as you would Jesus. Jesus promises to give His believers mercy, kindness, humility, gentleness, and patience.

Since God chose you to be the holy people He loves, you must cloth yourselves with tenderhearted, mercy. kindness, humility, gentleness, and patience. Colossians 3:12

God is always at work, guiding us to choose Him and to live through His word. He calls us to live by the teachings of the Holy Bible, for He is the one and only, the beginning and the end. Our Father is incredibly patient; He never gives up on us. He forgives our sins repeatedly. He is understanding, faithful, powerful, wise, and trustworthy. Our God is a true gentleman. He is our Father, our friend, and our family. *The Lord has made the heavens His throne from there He rules over everything. Psalms 103:19* He is our creator, our ruler. *How great is our Lord. His power is absolute His understanding is beyond comprehension. Psalms 147:5* He is perfect, He is eternal life. *Who else has held the oceans in His hand who has measured off the heavens with His fingers? Isaiah*

40:12 He is Almighty, His power is absolute. *I am the first and the last there is no other God. Isaiah 44:6.*

God sent His only Son to die on the cross for all the sins committed by humanity from the beginning to the end of time. Jesus Christ is our Savior and our brother. As the Son of God, Jesus can do nothing on His own but only what He sees the Father do. So, Jesus explained *I tell you the truth the son can do nothing by himself. He does only what He sees the father doing. Whatever their father does the son also does. For the father loves the son and shows Him everything He is doing in fact the father will show Him how to do even greater works than healing this man. John 5:19.* Understanding our Holy Family is the first step in understanding our own identity. When we accept Jesus as our Savior, we are reborn into our new identity in Christ. By accepting Jesus as our Savior, we become children of God, our Father Almighty. *To all who believed Him and accepted Him, He gave the right to become children of God. John 1:12*

1 God = 3 person

The Father	The Son	The Holy Spirit
Gave creation commands. -Genesis 1:1- 3	*Destroyed The dividing wall between us and God.* -Ephesians 2:13-18	*Provides rebirth and renewal.* -Titus 3:5
Sent His son to safe us. -John 4:14	*Mediator between us and the father* -1 Timothy 2:5	*Teaches us.* -John 14:26
Adopts us into His Holy Family -Ephesians 1:5	*Lives as our example* -Peter 2:21	*Guides us into truth.* -John 16:13
He is our protector. -Psalms 18:2	*Gives us eternal life.* -John 10:28	*Raised Jesus from the dead.* -Romans 8:11
Sent the Holy Spirit to live in us. -John 14:16-17	*Ask His Father to send The Holy Spirit to all believers.* -John 14:16	*Names us as children of God.* -Romans 8:9

Now that we understand that God is the Creator of all living things and that Jesus is the Son of God and Mother Mary, we can begin to learn about our own identity in Christ. "Who I Am" in Christ our Lord. Learning our identity is not defined by what we do or have done. It is defined by what Jesus has done and will do for us. This is His love and grace, which we receive from choosing Him as Our Savior. This is the foundation of our spiritual being, our identity in Christ. Our identity in Christ is unchanging; He is the beginning and the end, and He is constant and steadfast. Being rooted in Him, our identity will be unchanging as He is. Jesus is a gentleman who patiently waits for us to respond to His call in all that He asks of us. He is trustworthy. You can talk to Him about anything, knowing that your secrets are safe with Him. He is your friend. *I no longer call you slaves because a master does not confide in His slaves. You are my friends since I have told you everything the father told me. John 15:15* He is dependable, when we ask, we receive, when we seek, we find, when we knock, doors open. *Keep on asking and you will receive, what you ask for, keep on seeking and you will find. Keep knocking and the door will be opened to you. Matthew 7:7*

Reflection

Ask and Receive, Seek and Find, Knock and Doors Open

List the things you ask to become.

List the things you seek to know.

List things (opportunities) you ask to be opened.

This will be powerful, to reflect on, in the different seasons of your life.

Make sure you date.

_____

_____

_____

_____

_____

_____

The Sacred Hearts of the Holy Family

Perfect Union of Mercy, with three hearts beating as one

**The Sorrowful &
Immaculate Heart
of Mother Mary**

**The Sacred &
Merciful Heart
of Christ**

**The Most Pure &
Chaste Heart
of Joseph**

Heart of Jesus, I adore Thee.

Heart of Mary, I implore Thee.

Heart of Joseph, pure and just.

In these three hearts, I place my trust.

Take time and reflect on what the Holy Family means to you and fill in their hearts with your vision, who they are to you, what role they play, and the encouragement they give along your faith journey.

Receiving our identity in Jesus Christ, our Savior, will come with obstacles. These challenges may include overcoming our past sins and the false beliefs we hold about ourselves and others. These are just a fragment of the obstacles the devil uses to steal our relationship with Jesus, kill our belief in our faith, and destroy our salvation.

To defeat obstacles along our path, we must follow Jesus, believing that He is our Savior. On our behalf, The Holy Spirit will guide us through these challenges, asking God to guide and protect us. God assures us that we are loved with a purpose, uniquely created with great intentions. *For we are gods masterpiece. He has created us new in Christ Jesus so we can do the good things He planned for us long ago. Ephesians 2:10*

He designed every detail of each of us. We are chosen to be part of His Holy Family. The Bible—a book and letter from God—tells us that we are His children. We are loved, forgiven, redeemed, blessed, provided for, and accepted as part of His Royal family. This is only possible because His only Son died on the cross for us, His chosen ones.

NEW BEGINNINGS

Identity in Christ.

Fill in the wings of the butterfly with ways, you will fill the hearts, and souls, of others. Being their guidance towards their New Beginnings in finding their identity in Christ.

Our identity is rooted in being a child of God, He never sleeps. He is always working on us. Shaping us in His image of perfection. Our identity is built on the foundation of faith and grace we received when we accepted God as our Savior. It is important to understand that our identity is not decided by our job titles, family names, the things we have done in our lives, or even the cherished roles we hold as spouses, parents, and grandparents. To seek Jesus and find your identity, you do not have to look far – He is right by your side, He lives in your heart, and you live in His, just as he promised to always be. *I know the Lord is always with me I will not be shaken for He is right beside me. Psalm 16:8* He never leaves us, He waits patiently for us to seek Him as our savior in Christ.

For we all have sinned and fallen short of glory of God and are justified freely by His grace through the redemption that is in Christ Jesus when He freed us from the penalty for our sins. Romans 3:23-24 We need to repent our sins and be baptized in the Holy Spirit to receive forgiveness. Before I found my Identity in Christ, I always worried about what others thought or said about me. This would lead me to not having a desire to receive forgiveness. I used to struggle with confession, believing I could simply tell God my sins while in the shower and He would forgive me – and I do believe He does. However, there is profound power in the act of forgiveness and penance, the Sacrament of Reconciliation. This moment, hearing in your own voice, recalling your sins, in His presence, in His Holy Church. On your behalf, The Priest prays for forgiveness from God. *Each of you must repent of your sins and turn to God and be baptized in the name of Jesus Christ for the forgiveness of your Sins. Then you will receive gift of the Holy Spirit. Acts 2:38*

Jesus's identity

Who am I to you? Who do you believe I am?

Use the lines of Jesus to describe the things that forms

His identity in your eyes.

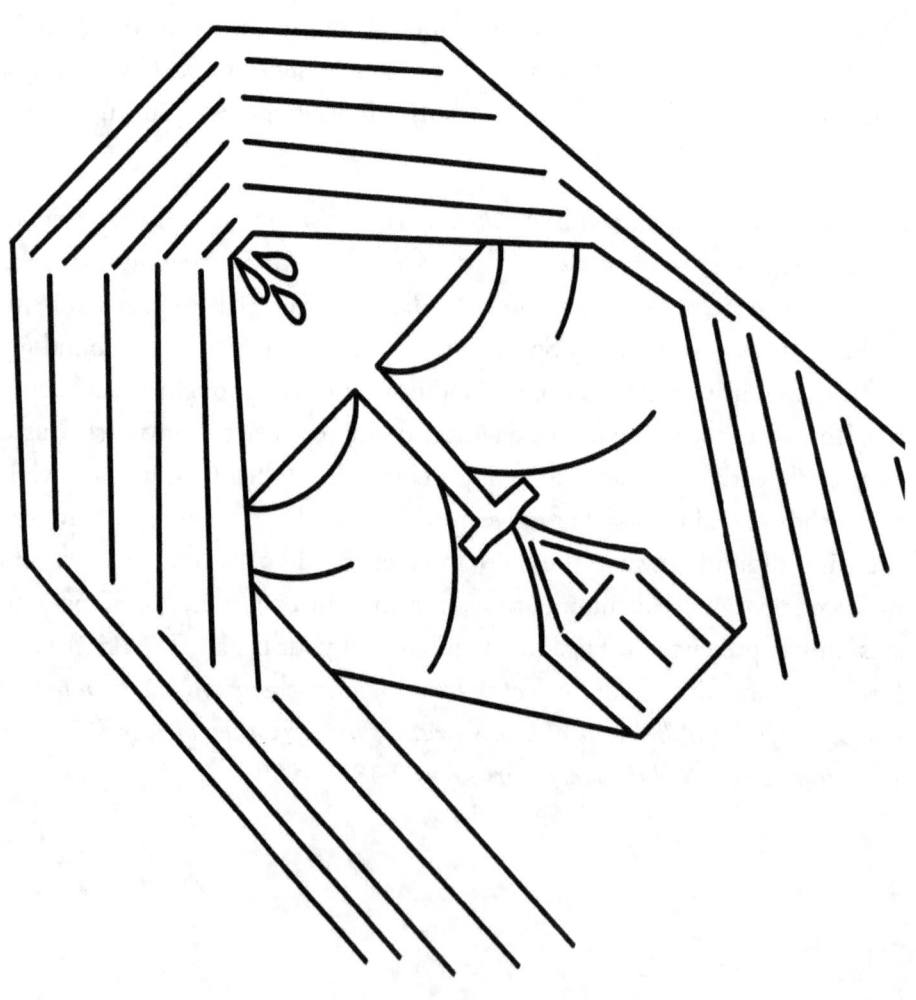

But who do you say I am?
Matthew 16:15

Vice (sins)

Habit that inclines someone to sin

Virtues (strength)

Behavior showing high moral standards

Pride Believing you are the source of your Own greatness	**Humility** Understanding that your gifts are from God
Envy Resenting others	**Kindness** Wish the best for others
Lust Treat others as mere objects sexual	**Chastity** Valuing dignity of others pure thoughts
Anger Negative emotions wish for revenge	**Meekness** Patience & charity when resolving issues
Gluttony Consuming to unhealthy excess	**Temperance** Take all things in moderation
Greed Unnecessary desire	**Generosity** Freely giving
Sloth Laziness avoids spiritual or physical work	**Diligence** Following Gods will

Sin

Sin is an act of offense against God by despising His person and Christian biblical law. Bring to life your sins. Fill the page by listing your sins. Tear out the page and set it on fire.

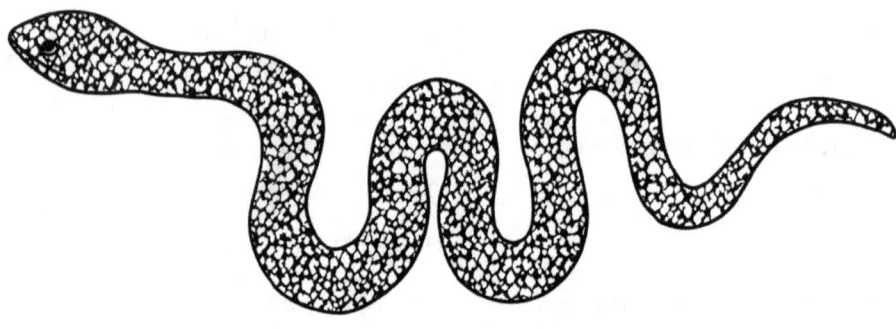

For the wages of sin is death; but the grace of God, life everlasting is Christ Jesus Our Lord. Romans 6:23

_____

_____

_____

_____

God made us and made us good. If you are a parent, think about how often you forgive your children for their words or for how they made you feel. If you are not a parent, consider the number of times you have forgiven your parents for not allowing you to do something or for not giving you what you thought you needed. We also forgive others for forgetting our special days or for not calling when we needed them most. Imagine all the times God forgives each of us for all our sins. He wants a relationship with us even more than we want one with Him. I hunger and thirst daily for more in my relationship with Him. I want more today than yesterday. Lord, I am longing for more of your salvation, for I want to do what pleases you. It is mind-blowing to realize just how much He wants a relationship with us. He has been seeking this relationship since He created us in His image and has never given up. He forgives our sins and remembers them no more. *For I will forgive their iniquity, and I will remember their sin no more. Jeremiah 31:34*

It is important to give Him our sins that prevent us from genuinely believing in Him. *If we confess our sins, He is faithful and righteous to forgive our sins and to cleanse us from all unrighteousness. John 1:19.* He tells us to give all our worries to Him and trust Him with them. Ask Him to guide you, in believing what He says about you, to be the truth. *And now dear brothers and sisters one fi nal thing fix your thoughts on what is true, honorable, right, pure, lovely, and admirable. Think about things that are excellent and worthy of praise. Keep putting into practice all you learned and received from me everything you heard from me and saw me doing then the God of peace will be with you. Philippians 4:8-9* When we put our faith in Jesus, we receive grace. Through this grace, we discover our identity in Christ. By receiving grace, our faith in our Lord Jesus Christ is renewed and strengthened. God sent His only begotten Son, Jesus, to die on the cross to provide salvation for all of us. *He canceled the certificate of debt consisting of decrees against us, which stood against us: He took it away, nailing it to the cross. Colossians 2:14* For this is how God loved the world: He gave His one and only Son so that everyone who believes in Him will not perish but have eternal life. We cannot achieve salvation without Jesus being our Savior. Praise His Holy Name for granting us grace and forgiveness of our sins, through His sacrifice on the cross. As we build a stronger relationship with Jesus, we will grow to resemble Him more and become less like who others perceive us to be. *You must have the same attitude that Christ Jesus had. Philippians 2:5* We are children of the highest Father Almighty. The King of Kings, The Lord of Lords.

OUR IDENTITY IN CHRIST

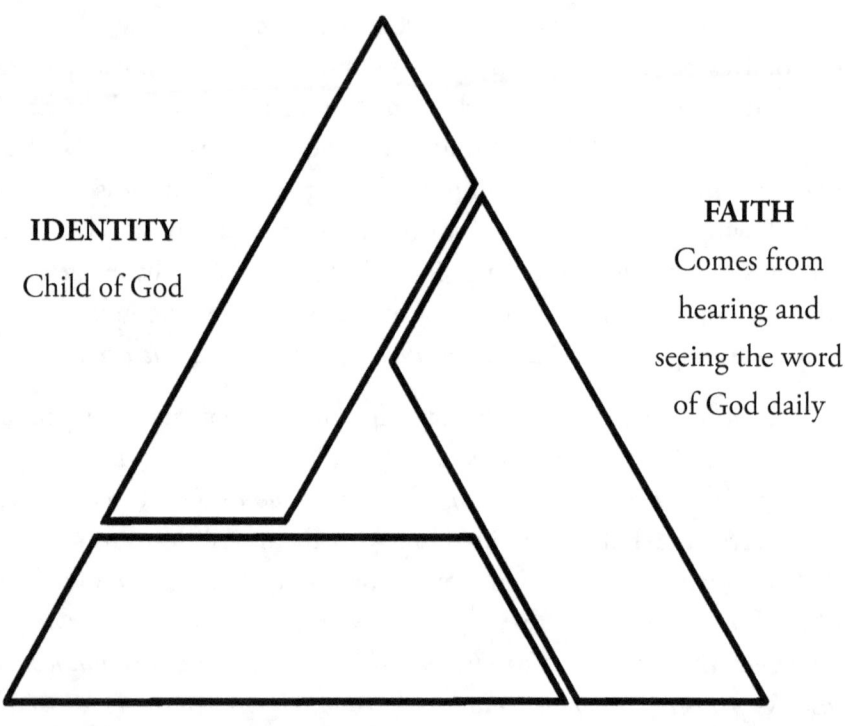

IDENTITY

Child of God

FAITH

Comes from
hearing and
seeing the word
of God daily

GRACE

Empowerment to do
what was impossible
without our God

And as we live in God our love grows more perfect. So, we will not be afraid on the day of judgment, but we can face Him with confidence because we live like Jesus here in this world. 1John 4:17

Jesus stands at your door.

Will you welcome Him in? Do you hear Him calling your name?

You alone, must ask Him to open the door, and come in.

You must seek, your intimate relationship, with the Lord, to hear His voice.

Behold I stand at the door and knock, if anyone hears my voice and opens the door, I will come in to Him and eat with Him and He with me. Revelation 3:20

Our religious identity is defined by how we see ourselves as children of God and how we uphold His values. This identity is given to us by God. We should remind ourselves we are part of The Holy Family. When we embrace our identity in Christ, we are gifted with authority, salvation, and the gifts of the Holy Spirit. With this identity, we gain complete access to Jesus, God the Father, The Holy Spirit, and Mother Mary. We receive our heritage by asking and receiving, seeking and finding, knocking, and having the door opened to us. *Keep on asking, and you will receive what you ask for, keep on seeking, and you will find. Keep on knocking and the door will be opened to you. For everyone who asks, receives. Everyone who seeks finds. And to everyone who knocks the door will be opened. Matthew 7:7-8*

To have an identity in Christ is believing, and living the word of God. To live like Him, to be more like Him and less like us. You must have the same attitude that Christ Jesus has. *Though He was God He did not think of equality of God as something to cling to. Instead, He gave up His divine privileges He took the humble position of a slave and was born as a human being. When He appeared in human form, He humbled Himself in obedience to God and died a criminal's death, on a cross. Philippians 2:6-8.* He calls us to follow Him, to praise and worship Him. God assures us that He is always with us and that everything He is, He is within us. We are worthy of all that belongs to Him. We have access to everything, we will ever need to fulfill, His grand plan for us. *By His divine power, God has given us everything we need to choose to live a Godly life. We have received all things, by coming to know Him, the one who called us, to Himself, by His marvelous glory, and excellence. And because of His glory, and excellence He has given us, great and precious promises. These are promises, that enable you, to share His divine nature, and escape the worlds corruption, caused by human desires. 2 Peter 1:3-4.* We must share His values with others and incorporate them into our daily routine. *Written not with ink but with the Spirit of the living God, not on tablets of stone but on tablets of human hearts. 2 Corinthians 3:3* By doing so, a fruitful ministry flows out of us, and touches the hearts, and souls, of others. Transformed people transform people leading them toward Heaven. Through my transformation, God has placed me in the presence of His children, who were seeking comfort. He has led me to share encouraging words, prayers, healing, time, love, and patience, to name just a few. Once we allow ourselves to be transformed in His image

42

and become His children, receiving His love. His Love is an indescribable love. A love you never knew you were missing. You become more like Him, in all you do and say, you hunger, not only for His love but for, His calling, for you to share His love to others. *What is the price of five sparrows two copper coins? Yet God does not forget one of them and the very hairs on your head are all numbered. So do not be afraid you are more valuable to God than a whole flock of sparrow. I tell you the truth everyone who acknowledges me publicly here on earth, the Son of Man will also be acknowledge in the presence of Gods angels.* Luke 12: 6-7

Identity + Intimacy = Lifestyle

IDENTITY	INTIMACY	LIFESTYLE
I am a child of God	Faith comes 1st.	We receive according. to our faith.
I have Righteousness	Grace from believing.	Live as Jesus lived
I do delight in the Lord	Ministry of our calling	Love as Jesus loved

Spreading His word glorifies Him. *So, whether you eat or drink or whatever you do it all for the glory of God. 1 Corinthians 10:31 God says the poor gives away and becomes rich. Our hearts ache but we always have joy. We are poor but we give spiritual riches to others. We own nothing and yet we have everything. 2 Corinthians 6:10* When giving, offer prayers, love, patience, compassion, time, actions, and scriptures, and shine your light on others. I have always lived to do for others, thinking I must buy them things to make them feel special. Living as a Child of God, my life is so much clearer. I now understand others want our time and our presence more than any materialistic items. *Share your food with the hungry and give shelter to the homeless give cloths to those who need them and do not hide from relatives who need your help. Isaiah 58:7.* God gives us everything we need with no price attached. You never know what battles the stranger next to you might be facing. Love as Jesus loves, for He loved first. Strengthen your faith in Jesus daily by seeing and hearing His word. Feed the hungry, cloth the naked, and provide shelter for the homeless. Forgive as Jesus forgives. *I yes, I alone will blot out your sins for my own sake and will never think of them again. Isaiah 43:25.* Be a godly example to everyone you meet throughout your day. We cannot change others or make them follow Jesus that is God's job alone. However, we are commanded to show God's love and share His promises in everything we do. When we walk in faith with love, our faith blossoms and shines onto others. A simple smile, a warm hello, a heartfelt thank you, or a kind "you're welcome" can brighten someone's day. Our true freedom comes when we learn to receive God's love and freely give it away. *Freely you have received: freely give. Matthew 10:8* But now you are free from the power of sin and are welcomed as slaves of God. *Now you do those things that lead to holiness and result in eternal life. Romans 8:15* Now, our identity is rooted in our intimacy relationship with God, living out our faith, grace, and ministry through acts of service to others. The acts of kindness He has called me to fill my heart with so much joy. Performing His work has more value to my identity than anything I have ever bought for others, with a price. Being present in the company of the broken-hearted and lost souls, giving prayer and clarification from God, has truly transformed my heart, mind, and soul. The gift God has entrusted in me has completely transformed my way of life. I have learned that I do not have a desire for materialistic things, and I no longer wish for acceptance from others. I cherish my time with our Lord daily. I want to be in His presence and to hear His voice. To grow in our identity with Jesus, we must praise Him, adore Him, and glorify Him. We are called to serve not to be served. *For even the son of men came not to be served but to serve, and to give His life as a ransom for many. Mark 10:45*

Growing in God's Love

Use the waterfall background on the next page to list:

- Ways you plan to share with others along your faith journey.

- Ways you plan to restore your neighbor's broken heart, lack of faith, or loneliness.

Having a contract with yourself and God will keep you accountable to live through His word daily. **Date**

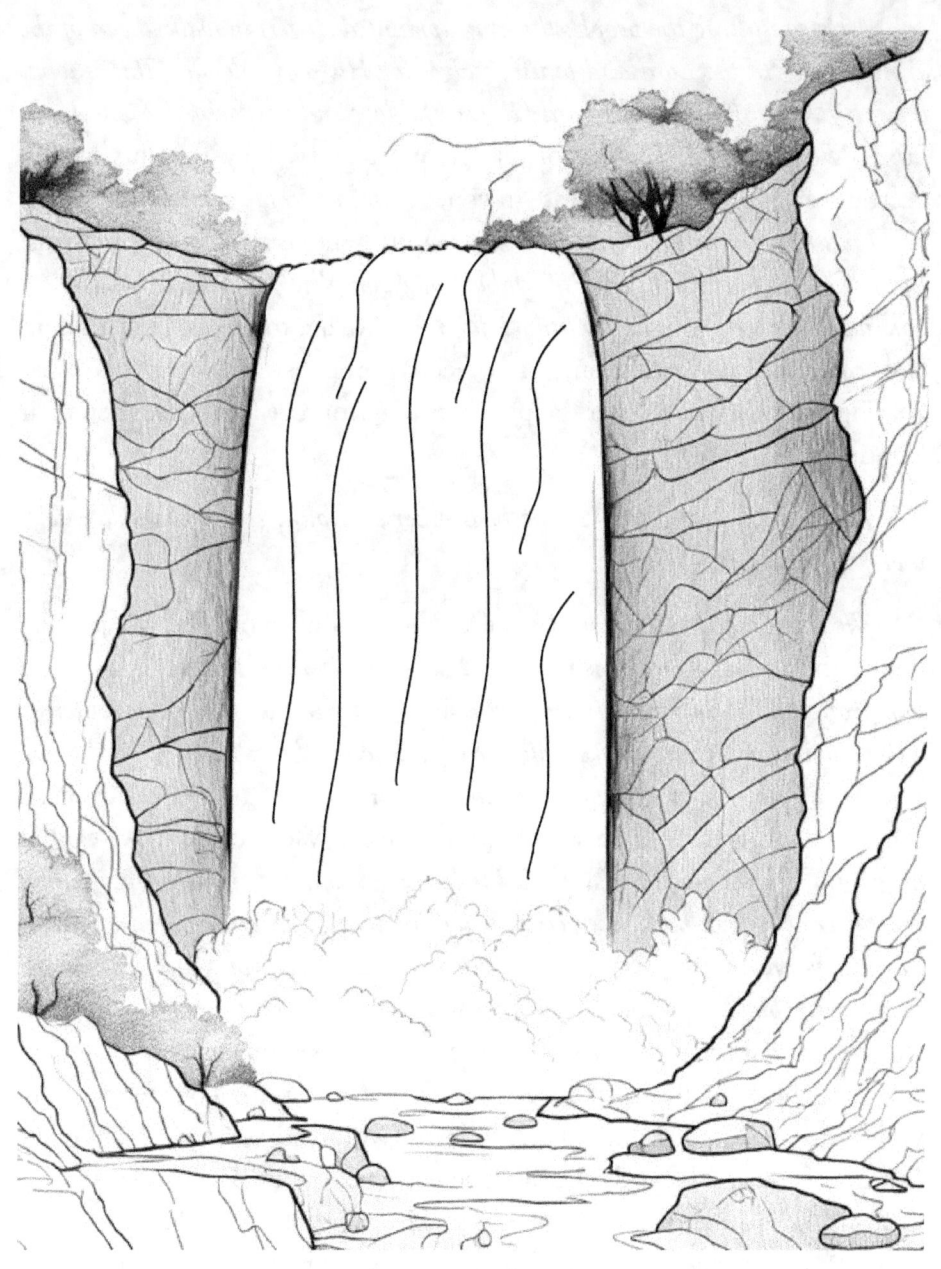

A generous person will prosper, whoever refreshes others will be refreshed.
Proverbs 11:25

After consulting the people, the king appointed singers to walk ahead of the army singing to the Lord and praising Him for His holy splendor This is what they sang: Give thanks to the Lord His faithful love endures forever! 2 Chronicles 20:21 We give Him thanks for all His great glory. Pray for ourselves to decrease, and for Him to increase in you. *He must become greater and greater, and I must become less and less. John 3:30* Overintense is our job as Christians. *But those who obey Gods word truly show how completely they love him. That is how we know we are living in him. 1 John 2:5* We are to be obedient to Him and follow in His word. Some are called to prophesy His word to others. Sharing His word with others helps others to encourage and strengthen their identity in the Lord.

But one who prophesies strengthens others, encourages them and comforts them. 1 Corinthians 14:3

We are to accept Jesus as Our Lord and Saviour in our life. We joyfully receive the blessings God has for us. *He says, I will rescue, those who love me, I will protect, those who trust in my name. When they call on me, I will answer, I will be with them in trouble, I will rescue and honor them. I will reward them, with a long life, and give them my salvation. Psalm 91: 14-15.* Have faith in all things of God to receive answers to your prayers. Without faith, we cannot expect our prayers to be answered. *I tell you; you can pray for anything. and if you believe that you have received it. It will be yours. But when you are praying first forgive anyone you are holding a grudge against so that your Father in heaven will forgive your sins. Mark 11:24-25* The stronger our faith becomes through studying and sharing the Word, the more we will see our prayers answered. We must always be moving forward on the path of building our relationship with Jesus to form our identity in Christ. We must carry our cross daily, continuing the road ahead, no matter the number of potholes, straightaways, or turns. Do not detour, stay on the path He leads you down. Feed our souls with His knowledge and wisdom daily to stay on the path of righteousness. We are called to help others carry their cross when they are struggling. *Carry each other's burdens, and in this way, you will fulfill the law of Christ. Galatians 6:2*

Show me the right path, O LORD point out the road for me to follow. Lead me by your truth and teach me, for you are the God who saves me. Psalm 25:4-11

Hold yourself accountable for your own actions. When you run off the road, put your foot on the brake and sit awhile, feel His presence, hear His voice. Follow His lead! *Trust in the Lord with all your heart and lean not on your own understanding: in all your ways submit to him, and He will make your paths straight. Proverbs 3:5-6*

Stay on the Road Ahead

Plan to grow daily in your faith with Christ. Hold yourself accountable, stay on the road that leads you to Enteral Life in Heaven. Fill in the signs with things you will add to your life to grow stronger in your faith. Daily Mass, Adoration, Volunteer Work?

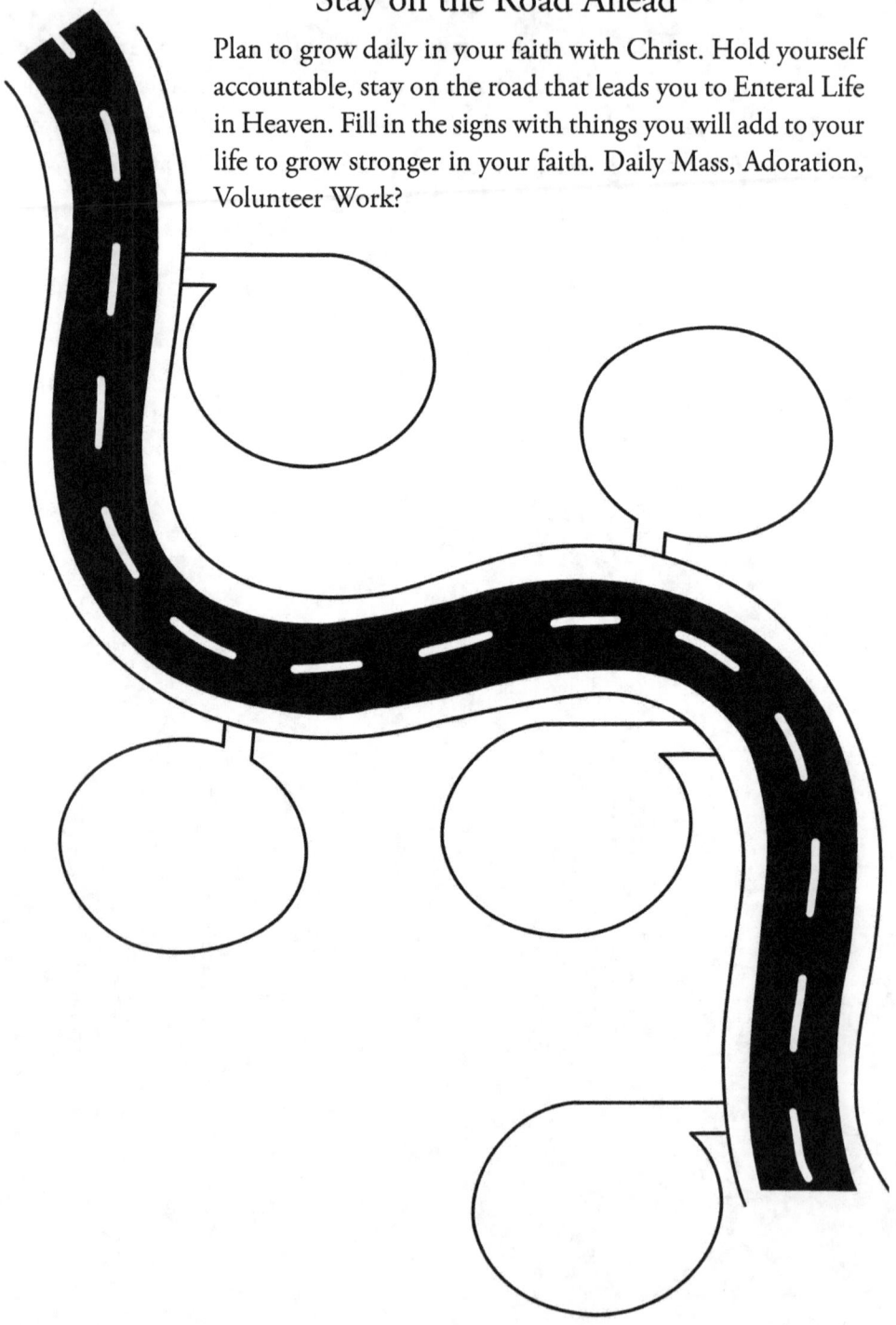

Feed the hungry, cloth the naked, and home the homeless. I have grown in my faith and identity by understanding God's calling to feed, cloth, and home His lost children. *Whoever is kind to the poor lends to the LORD, and He will reward them for what they have done. Proverbs 19:17* This message from God tells us that we are commanded to love others as He loves us, demonstrating this not just with material things but with prayer, love, time, patience, forgiveness, faith, scriptures, and communication—all of which are free and not bound by money. *So now I am giving you a new commandment Love each other Just as I have loved you. You should love each other. Your love for one another will prove to the world that you are my disciples John 13:34–35.*

These actions free our souls, strengthening our faith, grace, and identity, forming our intimate relationship with our Father. Building our faith also helps us accept the authority to make positive changes in our lives. As your faith grows stronger, you will notice changes in your prayer life, your moral values, your friendships, and even your health—just as I have experienced. Before I started my journey, I was always in and out of the doctor's office, on so much medication I could not keep up with what was what. It had gotten so bad I was starting to pass out and would have to be taken by ambulance to the ER. When I received the Holy Spirit, I felt all that pain at one time, and that was the last time. I am off all medication and enjoy going to the gym for a good workout. Not only has my soul, mind, and heart grown with God's love so has my physical body. *I pray that from His glorious unlimited resources He will empower you with inner strength through His spirit. Then Christ will make His home in your hearts as you trust in him. Your roots will grow down into God's love and keep you strong. Ephesians 3:16–17* The power of the Holy Spirit alive inside of you changes you from the inside out. Everything you study or read of God's word you understand on new heights, like you have known it your whole life. Learning the word of our savior and acting on the gifts I received from the Holy Spirit has completely transformed me, my whole body, mind, and soul. I received the Holy Spirit for the first time as a forty-six-year-old in the back of my brother's bar, where I was helping in the kitchen. So, if you can imagine, I had no high hopes of receiving anything from these ladies coming to pray over me. Little did I know how powerful the Holy Spirit truly is. From hearing the band playing and wondering how I would focus on them praying to resting in the Spirit. ***My transformation in the Holy Spirit was in the back of a Bar.*** Let's just say I do, believe in the power of the Holy Spirit. *God has given us the Spirit of His Son, and Jesus declares that His Father loves to give the Holy Spirit to those who ask. Galatians 4:6*

Our identity is built on our foundation of our authority in our Faith. Living out the words that God says are true about us, builds our faith. There are many ways to build our faith, like keeping our promises to the Lord, and spreading His word. *But how can they call on Him to save them unless they believe in him? And how can they believe in Him if they have never heard about him? And how can they hear about Him unless someone tells them and how will anyone go and tell them without being sent? That is why the scriptures say How beautiful are the feet of messengers who bring good news! But not everyone welcomes the good news for Isaiah the prophet said Lord who has believed our message? So, faith comes from hearing that is hearing the good news about Christ. But I ask to have the people of Israel heard the Message Yes, they have: the message has gone throughout the earth and the words to all the world. Romans 10:14-18* Studying and memorizing the word of the Lord will help build your confidence in believing what God says about you is true. Reflect on this verse for a while. Sit and hear what God is saying to you, what He is asking you to be for others.

Pray with Him morning and night, give Him praise and glory. He is the beginning and the end, so He should be the first person we speak to when we wake and the last person we pray with before we rest. *Seek first the kingdom and His righteousness and all these things will be given to you as well. Matthew 6:33* As a wife and mom, this has always been my weakness, a major obstacle keeping me from my intimate relationship with God. Young and freshly out of High School, I became a wife and first-time mom. Learning how to be a wife and mom left little time to myself, meaning I left God out more times than not. I could never understand how I was supposed to put anyone above my children. I had it all wrong for all these years of putting my kids above my husband and God. My life is so much brighter now that I know that My God waited patiently for me to get it right. Throughout the day, we should talk to Him— in praise, in comfort, and in times of worry. He is your family, your most trustworthy friend, the best secret keeper of all. *You are my friends if you do what I command. John 15:14.*

Ask the Lord to guide you in strengthening the part of your relationship with Him that needs it the most. For me, the area I have focused on the most in my relationship with God has been learning to sit still, to sit quietly, and to sit patiently with Him. *I wait quietly before God, for my victory comes from him. Psalm 62:1* Be patient and take the time to sit with Him; the more you sit with Him, the clearer you will hear His voice. I now believe I have always heard His voice. I was just not obedient, trusting that He was hearing me. I was not living out the true order of my identity. I had to learn all over again how to be a daughter of Christ. Listen to what He wants to tell you.

Every human desires to be a listening ear, but we also hunger to be heard. I have come to the understanding that I, too, have longed to be heard by my family and friends. I have hungered to know I was being heard by God. Why would our Lord not have the same desire of being heard, for He too is human? He created us in His image, so all that He is, He is within us. See Him; He walks with us through the darkness.

Keep praying; He is working, so be obedient in your walk with him. *Jesus spoke to the people once more and said I am the light of the world. If you follow me, you will not have to walk in darkness because you will have the light that leads the life. John 8:12.* Keep being obedient and praying, repenting your sins and receiving the body of Christ, will bring you closer to him. You come closer as you learn God's heart, His character, and His love. Believe what He says about you is true. *So, God has given both His promise and His oath. These two things are unchangeable because it is impossible for God to lie. Hebrews 6:18*

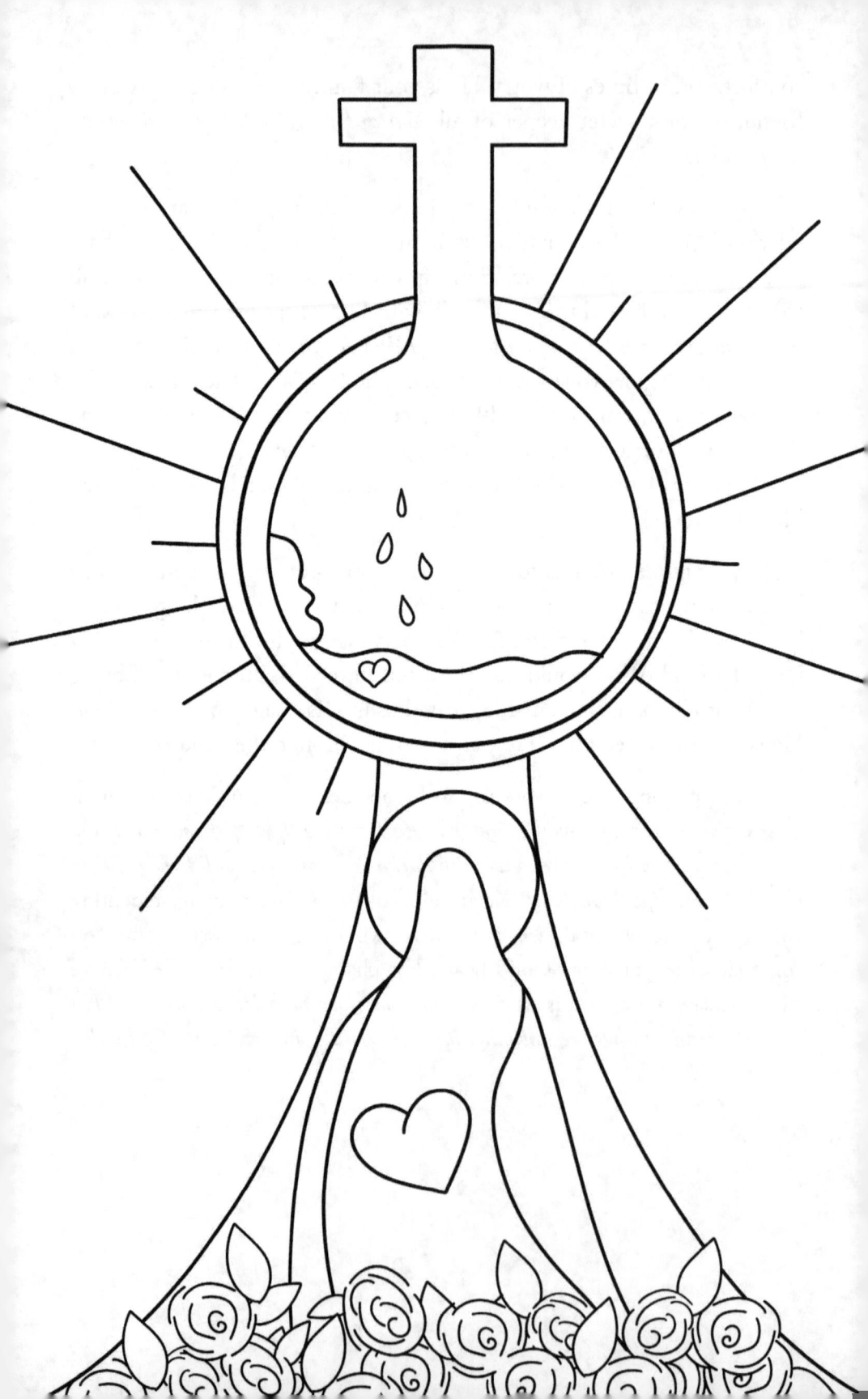

But it was to us that God revealed these things by His Spirit for His spirit searches out everything and shows us Gods deep secrets. No one can know a person thought except that person's own spirit and no one can know Gods thoughts except for Gods own spirit. And we have received Gods Spirit so we can know the wonderful things God has freely given us. 1 Corinthians 2:10-12 Fasting in prayer is a powerful way to free yourself of your own thoughts. Hear what He is saying. Take baby steps, start by giving up one thing at a time each week. *The psalmist says that fasting is a way to humble oneself before God. Psalm 35. To* desire more of Him, you must come to know more about who He is and what He says about Himself and about you. You need to understand who He is, and how He has formed you in His image.

Have true conversations with Jesus; He has been patiently waited to teach you through His parables.

Why do you use parables when you talk to people? His replied you are allowed to understand the secrets of the Kingdom of Heaven. But others are not. Those who listen to my teaching more understanding will be given, and they will have an abundance of knowledge. But for those who are not listening even what little understanding they have will be taken away from them. That is why I use these Parables. Matthew 13:10-13

God gives us authority as He has given to His son Jesus. *"Thanks be to God, who gives us the victory through our Lord Jesus Christ." 1 Corinthians 15:57 "Behold I have given you authority to trend on serpents and scorpions and over all power of the enemy and nothing shall hurt you." Luke 10:19.* We have the authority to rebuke the devil from our bodies and homes. This is important to understand for the closer you become to Him the stronger the devil will attack. Why do we often question God when terrible things happen to us or our loved ones? Should we not be blaming the devil when He trespasses into our lives for He comes to destroy? *Do not give the devil a foothold. Ephesians 4:27* Giving the devil a foothold or a tiny opening in our lives can open us up to sin. The devil surveys our lives, looking for any place to enter and take a hold on. Children of God are given the authority, through The Holy Spirit, to rebuke all evil from our lives and to grant forgiveness to others, ensuring the devil has no foothold over us. *"Submit yourself then to God resist the devil and He will flee from you." James 4:7*

God gives every believer the gift of the Holy Spirit. *Don't you realize that all of you together are the temple of God and that the Spirit of God lives in You? 1 Corinthians 3:16* The Holy Spirit played a massive role in my journey of finding my identity and hearing God's call, for my assignments as His daughter. *Believers receive gifts from God through the Holy Spirit. We receive the authority that comes with the gifts given to us from the spirit by God's orders. Three types of spiritual gifts are ministry gifts, manifestation gifts, and motivational gifts. God generously gives believers these gifts so we can exercise authority through the Holy Spirit which live within us. The manifestation of the spirit given for common good. One may receive wisdom, message of knowledge, faith, healing, miraculous powers, prophecy, distinguishing between spirits speaking in tongues, all are works of one spirit He distributes them to each one just as He finds fit. 1 Corinthians 12:811.* I have been blessed with multiple gifts in my newfound journey of faith, including prophecy, speaking in tongues, wisdom, and understanding. I have received the gift of prophecy twice, perhaps I was not perceiving in the way He was calling upon me. The second time, I was gifted with prophecy by The Holy Spirit through Father at the Encounter Conference. I was told that my words are like wrecking balls—when I speak, others will experience breakthroughs. This revelation has profoundly changed me into becoming a daughter of Christ. He calls me to share His words and healing with others more often than I ever thought I was worthy of.

Jesus came and told His disciples I have been given all authority in Heaven and on Earth Matthew 28:18. As part of The Holy Family we are a gifted heritage as His children. As believers of the royal family we have the authority to preach the Word of the Gospel to others. Our mission is given to us by Jesus Christ is to grow His kingdom here on Earth. If I had not been sharing His word during that late-night drive-through run, this book would not exist today. This book is proof that sharing His word is our mission. This was God's way of showing me the faith He has in me to prophesy His Word. Those who believe He is our true salvation have the authority to go directly to Him in prayer.

There for since we have been made right in Gods sight by faith, we have peace with God because of what Jesus Christ our Lord has done for us. Because of our faith Christ has brought us into this place of underserved privilege where we now stand, and we confidently and joyfully look forward to sharing Gods glory. Romans 5 1:2

We can petition God when we are in need of His mighty power. In doing so the answer may not always look the way we believe it should. Be reassured that God hears our prayers and answers them the way He sees fit at the time, in alignment with His timing. Believe in what you ask for, He cannot bless us with answered prayers until we accept Him as our savior. Ask for forgiveness, for your own sins and for the will to forgive others. We have the authority to ask for peace, healing and assurance in His name. As believers, we are gifted with the authority to help a broken world, not to harm it further. He calls us to embrace this authority wisely and correctly under His guidance. Through prayer and exercising our spiritual gifts, we can lead others closer to Him. God has entrusted us as His beloved children with this authority. We should use it wisely under His direction, seeking only His guidance to stay grounded in our faith.

Our Father in Heaven welcomes us as His beloved children with love and understanding. Through His love, our relationship with Him grew from the beginning of our journey and will continue till the end. In building your most important relationship with your Father. Stay strong in your belief in him, to grow, and do not leave any doors of anger, anxiety, depression, or unforgiveness open for the evil one to use as footholds to keep you from Our Lord Jesus Christ.

Share in God's values and incorporate them into your daily life. I pray that you build your faith in the love He has for you. He died for all of us to be fully and forever forgiven. He has given us a new identity as Children of Christ. You are a child of God, adopted into His Royal family with a rich heritage. Stay rooted in your love for God, in your faith, grace, and identity. Be obedient to the Lord, and you will receive a more heavenly mindset to live like Jesus. Surround yourself with godly people and things. Love yourself as you love others. Love as Jesus Loves. You are in His heart, and He, in yours. You are chosen! You are never alone. Continue to work on your relationship with your Savior more than anything else. Call on Him daily. Praise and Glorify His name. Open my eyes, Lord.

Let us pray,

God, we pray that we honor our identity in Your holy Name and that we come to fully recognize the beauty of being your beloved children. We praise and adore You. We thank you for the outpour of love and understanding that you place so gently on our hearts. You are our beginning and end, the only constant, never-changing love. Believing in all you say to be true. We pray that you help us to always stand strong in our identity as your beloved children. We pray that we continue to see the light you have placed ahead of us on our path to righteousness till we are called to enter your Heavenly Home. We pray that you continue to protect us from all the evil that seeks our souls and guide us in your word. We give you Thanks for all your answered and unanswered prayers for we trust in you Lord.

In Your Holy Name

Amen

Take time and write a contract with God of all your promises you want to be accountable for, in your newfound identity along your faith journey, be sure to date and sign:

Newfound Child of God

Our Father created you as a masterpiece, in His image.

He showed you that your identity is rooted in Christ alone.

- On the trunk, describe the foundation that God built your identity on.

- Use the branches to describe the qualities God used to create your identity.

- In the water, write the places you will go in your faith. Things God has placed on your heart to honor His Holy name.

Our new identity in Christ is a life of love, meaning and purpose. It is Christ living in and through us. God says identity is a sense of self that is durable and a sense of worth.

Quick Recap:

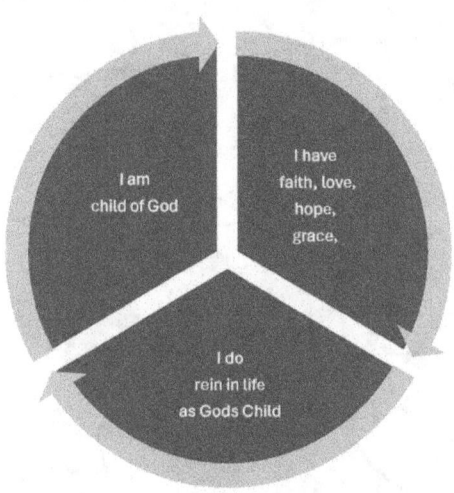

I am child of God

I have faith, love, hope, grace,

I do rein in life as Gods Child

Quick Review

- Child of God

Must have

to receive

- Intimate relationship with the Lord

- grace
- ministry
- faith

Bible Verses

From beginning to End

- *But one who prophesies strengthens others, encourages them, and comforts them.*
  Corinthian 14:3

- *My sheep listen to my voice; I know them, and they follow me. I give them eternal life, they will never perish no one can snatch them away from me.*
  John 10:27-28

- *Children are a gift from the Lord they are a reward from him.*
  Romans 8:15

- *Ye have not chosen me, but I have chosen you, and ordained you, that ye should go and bring forth fruit, and that your fruit should remain that whatsoever ye shall ask of the Father in my name, He may give it you.*
  John 15:16

- *Honor your father and mother that the days may be long in the land that the Lord your God is giving you.*
  Exodus 20:12

- *The Lord has done it this very day let us rejoice today and be glad.*
  Psalm 118:24

- *He must become greater and greater, and I must become less and less.*
  John 3:30

- *In returning and rest you shall be saved: in quietness and in trust shall be your strength.*
  Isaiah 30:15

- *Give thanks to the Lord for He is good His mercy endures forever.*
  Psalm 118:1

- *I will give thanks to the Lord with my whole heart: I will tell of all your wonderful deeds.*
  Psalm 9:1

- *His faithfulness and promises knowing He is working all things together for your good.*
  Romans 8:28

- *Seek the kingdom of God and His righteousness and all those things shall be added to you.*
  Matthew 6:38

- *I will give thanks to the Lord because of His righteousness I will sing the praises of the name of the Lord Most High.*
  Psalm 7:17

- *In the beginning God created the Heavens and Earth.* **Genesis 1:1** *Then God said 'Let there be light.* **Genesis 1:3** *Let the waters beneath the sky flow together into one place so dry ground may appear* **Genesis 1:9** *Let lights appear in the sky to separate the day from night.* **Genesis 1:14** *Let the waters swarm with fish and other life. Let the skies be filled with birds of every kind* **Genesis 20** *Let the earth produce each offspring of the same kind of livestock, small animal that scurry along ground and wild animals.* **Genesis 24** *Let us make human beings in our image to like us* **Genesis 26** *So God created human beings in His own image in the image of God He created them male and female.* **Genesis 27** *God blessed them and said Be fruitful and multiply fill the earth and govern it. Reign over the fish in the sea, the birds in the sky and all the animals that scurry along the grounds.* **Genesis 28** *Then God looked over all He had made, and He saw that it was exceptionally good.* **Genesis 31**

- *Salvation is not a reward for the good things we have done, so none of us can boast about it. For we are God's masterpiece. He has createed us anew in Christ Jesus, so we can do the good things He planned for us long ago.*
  Ephesians 2:9-10

- *So, you have not received a spirit that makes you fearful slaves. Instead, you received God's Spirit when He adopted you as His own children. Now we call Him Abba, Father.*
  Romans 8:15.

- *Even before He made the world God loved us and chose us in Christ to be holy and without fault in His eyes.*
  Ephesian 1:4

- *Because of our faith Christ has brought us into this place of underserved privilege where we now stand, and we confidently and joyfully look forward to sharing Gods glory.*
  Romans 5:2.

- *That is why I said that people cannot come to me unless the father gives them to me.*
  John 6:65

- *The Son gives us eternal life,' I give them eternal life and they will never perish No one can swatch them away from me'.*
  John 10:28

- *The Holy Spirit guides us into the truth. when they said this, Pilate brought Jesus out to them again The Pilate sat down on judgment seat on platform that is called the stone Pavement.*
  John 19:13

- *He lives as our example For God called you to do good even if it means suffering, just as Christ suffered for you. He is your example, and you must follow in His steps.*
  1 Peter 2:21

- *Since God chose you to be the holy people He loves, you must cloth yourselves with tenderhearted, mercy. kindness, humility, gentleness, and patience.*
  Colossians 3:12

- *The Lord has made the heavens His throne from there He rules over everything.*
  Psalms 103:19

- *He is all powerful. How great is our Lord. His power is absolute His understanding is beyond comprehension.*
  Psalms 147:5

- *He is perfect. Who else has held the oceans in His hand who has measured off the heavens with His fingers?*
  Isaiah 40:1

- *Our God He is eternal. I am the first and the last there is no other God.*
  Isaiah 44:6.

- *Jesus explained I tell you the truth the son can do nothing by himself. He does only what He sees the father doing. Whatever their father does the son also does. For the father loves the son and shows Him everything He is doing in fact the father will show Him how to do even greater works than healing this man.*
  John 5:19

- *To all who believed Him and accepted Him He gave the right to become children of God.*
  John 1:12

- *I no longer call you slaves because a master does not confide in His slaves. You are my friends since I have told you everything the father told me.*
  John 15:15

- *He is dependable, when we ask, we receive, when we seek, we find, when we knock doors open. Keep on asking and you will receive what you ask for keep on seeking and you will find. Keep knocking and the door will be opened to you.*
  Matthew 7:7

- *For we are gods masterpiece. He has created us new in Christ Jesus so we can do the good things He planned for us long ago.*
  Ephesians 2:10

- *I know the Lord is always with me I will not be shaken for He is right beside me.*
  Psalm 16:8

- *For we all have sinned and fallen short of glory of God and are justified freely by His grace through the redemption that is in Christ Jesus when He freed us from the penalty for our sins*
  Romans 3:23-24

- *Each of you must repent of your sins and turn to God and be baptized in the name of Jesus Christ for the forgiveness of your Sins Then you will receive gift of the Holy Spirit.*
  Acts 2:38

- *But who do you say I am?*
  Matthew 16:15

- *For the wages of sin is death; but the grace of God, life everlasting is Christ Jesus Our Lord.*
  Romans 6:23

- *For I will forgive their iniquity, and I will remember their sin no more.*
  Jeremiah 31:34

- *If we confess our sins, He is faithful and righteous to forgive our sins and to cleanse us from all unrighteousness.*
  John 1:19

- *And now dear brothers and sisters one final thing fix your thoughts on what is true, honorable, right, pure, lovely, and admirable. Think about things that are excellent and worthy of praise. Keep putting into practice all you learned and received from me everything you heard from me and saw me doing then the God of peace will be with you.*
  Philippians 4:8-9

- *He canceled the certificate of debt consisting of decrees against us, which stood against us: He took it away, nailing it to the cross.*
  Colossians 2:14

- *You must have the same attitude that Christ Jesus had.*
  Philippians 2:5

- *And as we live in God our love grows more perfect. So, we will not be afraid on the day of judgment, but we can face Him with confidence because we live like Jesus here in this world.*
  1 John 4:17

- *Behold I stand at the door and knock, if anyone hears my voice and opens the door, I will come in to Him and ear with Him and He with me.*
  Revelation 3:20

- *Keep on asking and you will receive what you ask for keep on seeking and you will find. Keep on knocking and the door will be opened to you. For everyone who asks, receives. Everyone who seeks finds. And to everyone who knocks the door will be opened.*
  Matthew 7:7

- *Though He was God He did not think of equality of God as something to cling to. Instead, He gave up His divine privileges He took the humble position of a slave and was born as a human being When He appeared in human form, He humbled Himself in obedience to God and died a criminal's death on a cross.*
  Philippians 2:68

- *By His divine power God has given us everything we need to choose to live a Godly life. We have received all things by coming to know Him the one who called us to Himself by His marvelous glory and excellence. And because of His glory and excellence He has given us great and precious promises These are promises that enable you to share His divine nature and escape the worlds corruption caused by human desires.*
  2 Peter 1:3-4

- *Written not with ink but with the Spirit of the living God, not on tablets of stone but on tablets of human hearts.*
  2 Corinthians 3:3

- *What is the price of five sparrows two copper coins? Yet God does not forget one of them and the very hairs on your head are all numbered So do not be afraid you are more valuable to God than a whole flock of sparrow. I tell you the truth everyone who acknowledges me publicly here on earth the Son of Man will also be acknowledge in the presence of Gods angels.*
  Luke 12: 6-7

- *So, whether you eat or drink or whatever you do it all for the glory of God.*
  1 Corinthians 10:31

- *God says the poor gives away and becomes rich. our hearts ache but we always have joy. We are poor but we give spiritual riches to others. We own nothing and yet we have everything.*
  2 Corinthians 6:10

- *I yes, I alone will blot out your sins for my own sake and will never think of them again.*
  Isaiah 43:25

- *Share your food with the hungry and give shelter to the homeless give cloths to those who need them and do not hide from relatives who need your help.*
  Isaiah 58:7

- *Freely you have received: freely give.*
  Matthew 10:8

- *Now you do those things that lead to holiness and result in eternal life.*
  Romans 8:15

- *For even the son of men came not to be served but to serve, and to give His life as a ransom for many.*
  Mark 10:45

- *A generous person will prosper whoever refreshes other will be refreshed.*
  Proverbs 11.25

- *After consulting the people, the king appointed singers to walk ahead of the army singing to the Lord and praising Him for His holy splendor This is what they sang: Give thanks to the Lord His faithful love endures forever!*
  2 Chronicles 20:21

- *He must become greater and greater, and I must become less and less.*
  John 3:30

- *But those who obey Gods word truly show how completely they love him. That is how we know we are living in him.*
  1 John 2:5

- *But one who prophesies strengthens others encourages them and comforts them*
  Corinthians 14:3

- *He says I will rescue those who love me I will protect those who trust in my name When they call on me, I will answer I will be with them in trouble I will rescue and honor them I will reward them with a long life and give them my salvation.*
  Psalm 91: 14-15

- *I tell you; you can pray for anything. and if you believe that you have received it. It will be yours. But when you are praying first forgive anyone you are holding a grudge against so that your Father in heaven will forgive your sins.*
  Mark 11:24-25

- *Carry each other's burdens, and in this way, you will fulfill the law of Christ.*
  Galatians 6:2

- *Show me the right path, O LORD point out the road for me to follow. Lead me by your truth and teach me, for you are the God who saves me.*
  Psalm 25:4-11

- *Whoever is kind to the poor lends to the LORD, and He will reward them for what they have done.*
  Proverbs 19:17

- *Trust in the Lord with all your heart and lean not on your own understanding: in all your ways submit to him, and He will make your paths straight.*
  Proverbs 3:5-6

- *So now I am giving you a new commandment Love each other Just as I have loved you. You should love each other. Your love for one another will prove to the world that you are my disciples.*
  John 13:34-35

- *God has given us the Spirit of His Son, and Jesus declares that His Father loves to give the Holy Spirit to those who ask.*
  Galatians 4:6

- *But how can they call on Him to save them unless they believe in him? And how can they believe in Him if they have never heard about him? And how can they hear about Him unless someone tells them and how will anyone go and tell them without being sent? That is why the scriptures say How beautiful are the feet of messengers who bring good news! But not everyone welcomes the good news for Isaiah the prophet said Lord who has believed our message? So, faith comes from hearing that is hearing the good news about Christ. But I ask to have the people of Israel heard the Message Yes, they have: the message has gone throughout the earth and the words to all the world.*
  Romans 10:14-18

- *Seek first the kingdom and His righteousness and all these things will be given to you as well.*
  Matthew 6:33

- *I wait quietly before God, for my victory comes from him.*
  Psalm 62:1

- *Jesus spoke to the people once more and said I am the light of the world. If you follow me, you will not have to walk in darkness because you will have the light that leads the life.*
  John 8:12

- *So, God has given both His promise and His oath. These two things are unchangeable because it is impossible for God to lie.*
  Hebrews 6:18

- *But it was to us that God revealed these things by His Spirit for His spirit searches out everything and show us Gods deep secrets. No one can know a person thought except that person's own spirit and no one can know Gods thoughts except for Gods own spirit. And we have received Gods Spirit so we can know the wonderful things God has freely given us.*
  1 Corinthians 2:10-12

- *The psalmist says that fasting is a way to humble oneself before God.*
  Psalm 35

- *Why do you use parables when you talk to people? His replied you are allowed to understand the secrets of the Kingdom of Heaven. But others are not. Those who listen to my teaching more understanding will be given, and they will have an abundance of knowledge. But for those who are not listening even what little understanding they have will be taken away from them. That is why I use these Parables.*
Matthew 13:10-13

- *Thanks be to God, who gives us the victory through our Lord Jesus Christ.*
1 Corinthians 15:57

- *Behold I have given you authority to trend on serpents and scorpions and over all power of the enemy and nothing shall hurt you.*
Luke 10:19

- *Do not give the devil a foothold.*
Ephesians 4:27

- *Submit yourself then to God resist the devil and He will flee from you.*
James 4:7

- *God gives every believer the gift of the Holy Spirit. Don't you realize that all of you together are the temple of God and that the Spirit of God lives in You?*
1 Corinthians 3:16

- *Believers receive gifts from God through the Holy Spirit. We receive the authority that comes with the gifts given to us from the spirit by Gods orders. Three types of spiritual gifts are ministry gifts, manifestation gifts, and motivational gifts. God generously gives believers these gifts so we can exercise authority through the Holy Spirit which lives within us. The manifestation of the spirit given for common good. One may receive wisdom, message of knowledge, faith, healing, miraculous powers, prophecy, distinguishing between spirits speaking in tongues all are works of one spirit He distributes them to each one just as He finds fit.*
1 Corinthians 12:8-11

- *Jesus came and told His disciples I have been given all authority in Heaven and on Earth.*
Matthew 28:18

- *There for since we have been made right in Gods sight by faith, we have peace with God because of what Jesus Christ our Lord has done for us. Because of our faith Christ has brought us into this place of underserved privilege where we now stand, and we confidently and joyfully look forward to sharing Gods glory.*
  Romans 5:1

Definitions

From beginning to End

- **Our Lord Jesus Christ-** *Jesus is God. Jesus has "all authority in heaven and on earth" He is Lord of the Sabbath. He is "our only Sovereign and Lord." He is, in fact, the Lord of lords The mother of Jesus, who was conceived through the Holy Spirit. She is referred to as the Virgin Mary in Catholic tradition because of the doctrine of her perpetual virginity. Mary is the only Virgin who is also a Mother. She was a daughter of the royal family, descended from David. After giving birth to Jesus in Bethlehem, she raised Him in the city of Nazareth in Galilee and was in Jerusalem at His crucifixion and with the apostles after His ascension.*

- **God-** *The supreme being and the creator of the universe. He is eternal, all-powerful, all-knowing, ever-present, unchanging, loving, just, merciful, gracious, and sovereign over all creation. His nature is described as spirit, light, love, and a consuming fire.*

- **The Holy Spirit-** *The presence of God that acts and dwells in our lives. The Holy Spirit unites believers with Christ and places them in the body of Christ, the church. The Holy Spirit lives inside believers and helps them grow closer to God. In Greek, the Holy Spirit is referred to as a spirit with the power of knowing, desiring, deciding, and acting.*

- **Instrument Of God-** Being an instrument of God means setting a good example to convince other people to change their way of life and have a sacred relationship with Him. To be a useful instrument for God, we have to know the 'what' and 'how' to act according to God's methods and principles. We are able to be true instruments of God by making a strong connection between us, Himself, and the Father in Heaven. Under the new covenant, the law of God is to be in the minds of His people, and we use our minds as instruments of righteousness by acquiring knowledge of God's word and understanding what He expects of us.

- **Child of God-** Being a child of God means that we are loved and cherished by God, who is our Father in heaven. It also means that we are protected and provided for by God, who will look after us as His children. Being a child of God requires us to live the Gospel, which makes us like the Father, and to forgive and share our gifts with others. Being a child of God is a result of being born a second time into God's family through Jesus Christ.

- **Spiritual Companion-** Someone who listens to you and guides you to discover what is already within you. They hold a sacred space for your relationship with God to deepen and broaden. Spiritual companionship is a relationship in which a companion allows, through deep listening, the spiritual story of the other to unfold. The companion is welcoming and present, listening and responding without being judgmental.

- **Trinity-** The Christian Godhead as one God in three persons: Father, Son, and Holy Spirit. A group of three people or things:

- **The Holy Royal Family-** Catholic tradition consists of the Child Jesus, the Virgin Mary, and Saint Joseph. The Feast of the Holy Family, celebrated on the first Sunday after Christmas, commemorates their life together and serves as a model for all Christian families.

- **Catholic Holy Church-** The Catholic Church is one, holy, catholic and apostolic church founded by Jesus Christ in His Great Commission

- **Holy Bible-** A collection of sacred books written by ancient prophets and historians, recording the relationship between God and His people for over 4,000 years. The term "Bible" can refer to the Hebrew Bible or the Christian Bible, which contains both the Old and New Testaments. It is considered the very Word of God and provides guidance on peace, hope, and salvation. The word "Bible" may have originated from the ancient Egyptian port of Byblos. In the Bible, "holy" refers to something or someone separated and dedicated to serve and fulfill the will of God.

- **Parables-** Simple stories used to illustrate a moral or spiritual lesson. Jesus used parables to teach important spiritual truths and to reveal and conceal spiritual truths. The spiritual sense of parables can be separated into its allegorical sense, its moral sense, and its anagogical sense. The allegorical sense recognizes the significance of events in Christ, the moral sense teaches us how to live as faithful Christians, and the anagogical sense leads us toward our true homeland.

- **Christian Biblical Law**- God's laws are the rules of the Kingdom of God and His way of life, and they are divine and perfect in intent, equity, and administration. The apostle Paul said God's "law is holy, and the commandment holy and just and good" as well as "spiritual."

- **Intimacy Relationship with God**- Here's the key to intimacy with God in a nutshell: spend dedicated time with Him daily through prayer and Bible study while also maintaining an awareness of His presence throughout your day. Having an intimate relationship with God requires making intentional time to connect with Him.

- **Faith**- Is a profound belief or trust in a higher power, divine presence, or universal consciousness. Faith, in a spiritual context, is not just about accepting a specific set of religious doctrines or practices. It is the spiritual practice of trusting and giving oneself over to something bigger than one's own self. Faith is seen as a relationship and involves an awareness of and an attunement to God's presence in our everyday experiences.

- **Grace**- Represents the unmerited favor and love of a higher power towards humanity. Is a divine influence that inspires virtuous behavior, imparts strength, and leads to spiritual growth. Is central to Christian belief, reflecting God's freely given, undeserved love and assistance. Enables individuals to overcome life's challenges and experience transformation. Is a gift that brings spiritual blessings, forgiveness, and salvation.

- **Salvation**- Refers to death and freedom from sin, a new perspective that transcends the human point of view, participation in a new creation, peace with God, life as adopted children of God, baptism into Christ's death, and the reception of the Holy Spirit. It also refers to spiritual and material preservation, deliverance from the fear of danger, pardon, restoration, healing, wholeness, and soundness in spirit, soul and body.

- **Temple-** Symbolizing God's dwelling place on earth Representing His presence, holiness, and relationship with His people. Serving as a place of worship, sacrifice, and connection to the divine. Being a sacred place where heaven and earth meet. In the Old Covenant, the temple was a physical building where people could worship God and God could speak to them.

- **Authority-** A divine attribute entrusted to individuals to carry out God's will. Rooted in divine order and God's sovereignty. Includes earthly authorities such as kings, priests, and leaders The freedom to decide or the right to act without hindrance. Delegated right to rule or lead, with the responsibility to bring about controls within the limits set by God.

- **Prophesy-** "to prophesy" is the verb. "a message from God." Hence, to prophesy is to declare a message from God.

- **Identity in Christ-** The biblical meaning of "identity in Christ" is central to Christian theology. It refers to the transformation and new identity a believer receives when they come to faith in Jesus Christ. In Christ, believers do not lose their true selves but rather become their true selves.

- **Vice-** Immoral or evil habit or practice. In Christian teachings, the seven deadly sins, also known as the capital vices or cardinal sins, are a grouping and classification of vices. The seven deadly sins are pride, greed, wrath, envy, lust, gluttony, and sloth, which are contrary to the seven capital virtues.

- **Virtues-** In the Bible, virtue refers to moral excellence and conformity to divine standards of righteousness and holiness. It encompasses qualities such as wisdom, courage, kindness, and self-control. Believers are called to pursue virtues and develop theological virtues of faith, hope, and love.

- **Sin-** A concept in Christianity that refers to an act that violates God's will. The seven deadly sins were initially listed as lust, idolatry, greed, discord, indulgence, wrath, and pride. In 590 CE, Pope Gregory I rewrote the list of sins, changing them to lust, gluttony, greed, sloth, envy, wrath, and pride. Virtue is a concept in Christianity that refers to a behavior that is morally good. The revised virtues became chastity, temperance, charity, diligence, kindness, patience, and humility. Other virtues include generosity, poverty of spirit, gentleness, purity of heart, temperance, and fortitude.

- **Confession-** Acknowledges sinfulness and is regarded as necessary to obtain divine forgiveness. Allows believers to seek forgiveness for their sins and reconcile with God. Rooted in the teachings of Jesus Christ and considered a fundamental aspect of Christian faith and spirituality. A confession of faith serves as a public declaration and affirmation of core beliefs and doctrines. Confession is the spiritual discipline that allows us to enter into the grace and mercy of God in such a way that we experience forgiveness and healing for the sins and sorrows of the past. Both forgiveness and healing are involved in confession.

- **Foothold-** Is based upon lies one believes that lead him/her into sin for which he/she remains unrepentant. Continuing to function in that sin gives Satan a place from which to advance against us—to gain more ground in our lives.

- **Free Will-** He gave us free will—the ability to think, reason, and make our own choices. He gives us commands and instructions that show us how He wants us to live, but He allows us to decide whether we will obey.

- **Adoration-** Eucharistic Adoration in the Catholic Church refers to the worship of the Eucharist outside of the Mass. During Adoration, the Eucharistic Host is displayed in a monstrance on the altar, allowing the faithful to pray in the presence of Christ. It is a way to be present with the Lord and actively listen to His word through prayer.

- **Image-** A physical representation of a person or thing. In the Old Testament, the words "image" (tselem) and "likeness" (demuth) are used to define man's fundamental relation to God.

- **Ignatian prayer-** The Ignatian Daily Examen is a prayer technique developed by St. Ignatius to help us reflect on the events of the day and discern God's presence and direction. It involves several steps, including thanksgiving, reviewing the day, talking with God, and looking ahead to tomorrow. A common prayer associated with this practice is: "Lord, grant that I may see you more clearly, love you more dearly, and follow you more nearly, day by day."

- **Augustinian prayer-** Unlike Ignatian prayer, in which you place yourself into the Gospel story, Augustinian prayer is a practical application of Scripture reading, pulling out of it what you find applies to your present circumstances as if the passage is personal communication from God.

- **Franciscan prayer-** A collection of prayers and devotions. The most famous of these is the Prayer of Saint Francis of Assisi, which is a prayer for peace and is often used in religious services and events. The prayer asks God to make the speaker an instrument of peace and to help them spread love, pardon, faith, hope, light, and joy. Other Franciscan prayers include the Prayer before the Crucifix, St. Francis' Testament Prayer, and the Peace Prayer of St. Francis.

- **Thomistic prayer-** An intellectual prayer life that depends on a neat, orderly approach. In prayer, Thomists will take a virtue, mystery of faith, or a theological truth and study it from every angle, asking: Who? What? When? Why? How? This leads them to deeper contemplation and dialogue with God. Thomistic prayer is mostly meditation and study mixed together. An examination of conscience is a Thomistic form of prayer.

- **Holy Rosary-** Christ-centered prayer in the Catholic tradition. It helps us meditate on the lives of Jesus and Mary, and we ask for the intercession of Mary, the Mother of God, in drawing closer to her divine Son, Jesus. The word "rosary" means "crown of roses" and reflects the idea of presenting a group of prayers to Mary as a spiritual bouquet. It is essentially a meditation on the life of Jesus and His Mother.

To Believe!

Jesus is my shepherd.

I hear His voice.

I am His beloved sheep.

I know His voice & He knows mine.

Hear His voice.

www.ingramcontent.com/pod-product-compliance
Lightning Source LLC
Chambersburg PA
CBHW071541120626
46550CB00006B/2532

* 9 7 9 8 8 9 3 2 4 5 9 8 1 *